THE WORLD'S WORST NATURAL DISASTERS

THE WORLD'S WORST
TORNADOES

by John R. Baker

raintree

a Capstone company — publishers for children

Raintree is an imprint of Capstone Global Library Limited, a company incorporated in England and Wales having its registered office at 264 Banbury Road, Oxford, OX2 7DY – Registered company number: 6695582

www.raintree.co.uk
myorders@raintree.co.uk

Edited by Aaron Sautter
Designed by Steve Mead
Picture research by Jo Miller
Production by Tori Abraham
Originated by Capstone Global Library Limited
Printed and bound in China

ISBN 978 1 474 72478 4
20 19 18 17 16
10 9 8 7 6 5 4 3 2 1

British Library Cataloguing in Publication Data
A full catalogue record for this book is available from the British Library.

Acknowledgements
We would like to thank the following for permission to reproduce photographs: AP Images, 18–19, Pavel Rahman, 12–13; Getty Images: AFP Photo/Ross Tuckerman, 22–23, Hulton Archive/Topical Press Agency, 6–7, Jerry Laizure, 8–9, Jordan Mansfield, 16–17, Zachary Roberts, 20–21; Newscom: EPA/Ken Blackbird, 24–25, UPI/Tom Uhlenbrock, 14–15, ZUMA Press/Ken Stewart, 10–11, ZUMA Press/ St Petersburg Times, 28–29; Shutterstock: EmiliaUngur, 4–5, leonello calvetti, cover, 3, 31, Martin Hass, cover, Minerva Studio, 26–27, solarseven, design elements, xpixel, design elements

CONTENTS

NATURE'S POWER UNLEASHED

THE EF SCALE

5
4
3
2
1
0

Tornadoes in the United States are ranked from 0 to 5 on the Enhanced Fujita (EF) Scale. In the UK, t
Tornado Intensity Scale. On both scales, the strongest tornadoes have the highest ranks.

Trees snapped in half. Roofs ripped off buildings. Cars tossed around like toys. What did this? A tornado! Every year, these powerful twisting storms cause damage around the world. Hang on tight. It's time to learn about the world's worst tornadoes.

RANKING

0	1	2	3	4	5
105 to 137 kph (65 to 85 mph)	138 to 177 kph (86 to 110 mph)	178 to 217 kph (111 to 135 mph)	218 to 266 kph (136 to 165 mph)	267 to 322 kph (166 to 200 mph)	322 kph (200 mph)

wind speeds (kilometres/miles per hour)

TRI-STATE TERROR

Location:
Missouri, Illinois
and Indiana, USA

Date:
18 March 1925

EF rating:

5
4
3
2
1
0

On 18 March 1925, one tornado set a record.
The monster twister stayed on the ground
for an incredible 352 kilometres (219 miles)!
It destroyed entire towns across three
US states. The Tri-State Tornado was the
deadliest in US history. It killed 695 people.

cyclone fast spinning column of air

MONSTER IN OKLAHOMA

Location:
Oklahoma City,
Oklahoma, USA

Date:
3 May 1999

EF rating:

5
4
3
2
1
0

On 3 May 1999, a giant, 1.6-kilometre- (1-mile-) wide tornado destroyed entire neighbourhoods in Oklahoma City, USA. Streets were filled with broken trees and shattered homes. The giant twister caused more than $1 billion worth of damage. It killed 36 people.

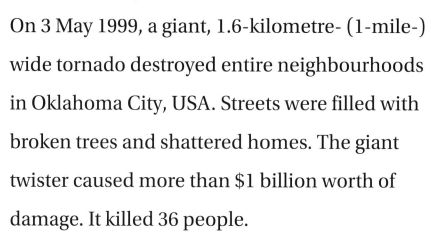

The Oklahoma City tornado had wind speeds of up to 512 kilometres (318 miles) per hour. It was the fastest tornado wind speed ever recorded.

1974 SUPER OUTBREAK

Location:
Midwest and eastern United States

Date:
3–4 April 1974

EF rating:

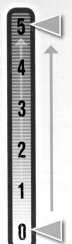

5
4
3
2
1
0

Huge storms swept across North America in April 1974. They created a record **outbreak** of more than 140 tornadoes. The twisters caused death and destruction in 13 US states and Canada. At least 65 of those twisters were rated EF3 or higher.

FACT

The 1974 Super Outbreak killed more than 300 people. The twisters also caused more than $600 million worth of damage.

outbreak large number of events that occur in a certain area

DISASTER IN BANGLADESH

Location:
Dhaka,
Bangladesh

Date:
26 April 1989

EF rating:

5 unknown
4
3
2
1
0

The world's deadliest tornado occurred on 26 April 1989. The killer twister hit near Dhaka, Bangladesh. About 1,300 people died as it tore through thousands of homes. Another 12,000 suffered injuries in the storm.

The deadly storm in Bangladesh left 80,000 people without homes.

A DIRECT HIT

Location:
Joplin, Missouri, USA

Date:
22 May 2011

EF rating:

5
4
3
2
1
0

On 22 May 2011, a giant EF5 tornado hit Joplin, Missouri, USA. The monstrous twister ploughed a path of destruction through the middle of the town. It killed more than 150 people. It also caused a record $2.8 billion worth of damage.

FACT

In April 2011, more than 750 tornadoes were recorded in the United States, setting a new record.

UK OUTBREAK

Location:
UK

Date:
23 November 1981

EF rating:

Nowhere in the world is safe from tornadoes. On 23 November 1981, a record 105 twisters hit the UK. There were 13 tornadoes recorded in Norfolk alone. Most of them were relatively weak and didn't last long.

Tornadoes in the UK are rated using the International Tornado Intensity Scale. The weakest storms have a T0 rating. The strongest are rated T11.

TOPEKA TWISTER

Location:
Topeka, Kansas, USA

Date:
8 June 1966

EF rating:

5
4
3
2
1
0

It was a **humid** summer day on 8 June 1966. That evening a giant EF5 tornado headed straight for Topeka, Kansas, USA. It tore a 35-kilometre- (22-mile-) long path through the city. The fierce storm damaged 3,000 homes. It killed 16 people. Another 500 were injured.

In 1912, Regina was a thriving city in Saskatchewan, Canada. On 30 June a tornado destroyed much of the city. The cyclone flattened homes. It reduced brick buildings to rubble. The twister left 2,500 people with nowhere to live.

FACT The Regina twister killed 28 people. That's more than any other tornado in Canada's history.

ONE POWERFUL STORM

Location:
Bucca, Australia

Date:
29 November
1992

EF rating:

5
4
3
2
1
0

22

Most tornadoes in Australia aren't very strong. But a powerful EF4 twister struck the small town of Bucca on 29 November 1992. It had wind speeds of 267 kilometres (166 miles) per hour. The storm also carried tennis-ball-sized **hail**. It was the strongest tornado ever seen in Australia.

FACT

On 4 November 1973, a tornado ripped up more than 1,300 buildings near Brisbane. It caused more damage than any other twister in Australia's history.

hail small pellets of ice that can fall during a thunderstorm

A SUPER-SIZED MONSTER

Location:
Hallam,
Nebraska, USA

Date:
22 May 2004

EF rating:

5
4
3
2
1
0

The widest twister ever recorded hit Hallam, Nebraska, USA, in 2004. This super-sized EF5 monster stretched 4 kilometres (2.5 miles) wide. Mud and **debris** from the small town's buildings filled the streets.

FACT

The Hallam tornado destroyed 150 homes. It also wiped out the town's schools, post office, churches and office buildings.

debris scattered pieces of something that has been broken or destroyed

A TORNADO FACTORY

Location:
south-eastern United States

Date:
15–18 September 2004

EF rating:

Hurricanes often form dozens of tornadoes. In 2004, Hurricane Ivan set a record for the most twisters created by a hurricane. When Ivan hit the south-eastern United States, it formed 117 tornadoes over four days.

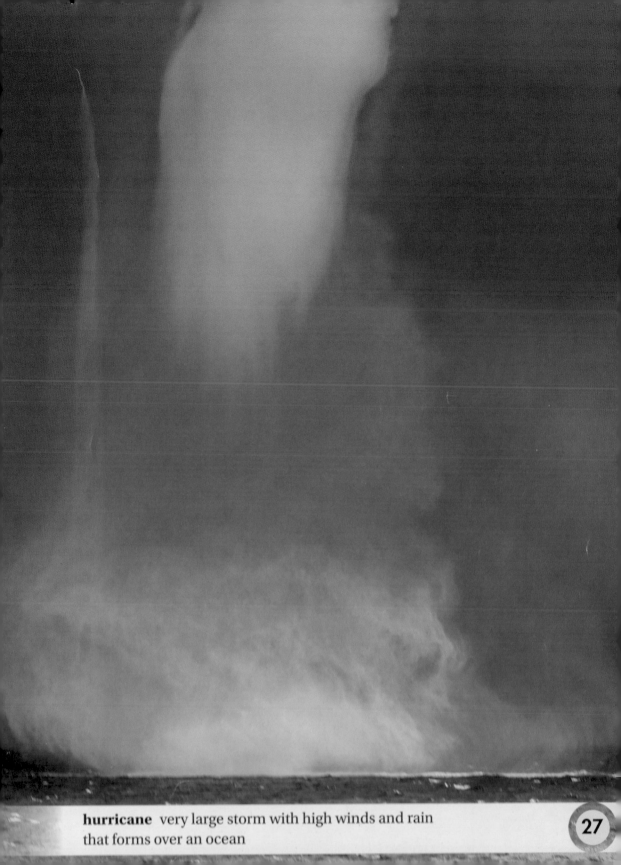

hurricane very large storm with high winds and rain
that forms over an ocean

TORNADO SAFETY

It's important to be prepared in places where tornadoes strike. When a **tornado warning** sounds, people need to head for the nearest storm shelter. They should stay in corridors and keep away from windows. Tornadoes are nature's fiercest storms. Knowing what to do can help keep people safe.

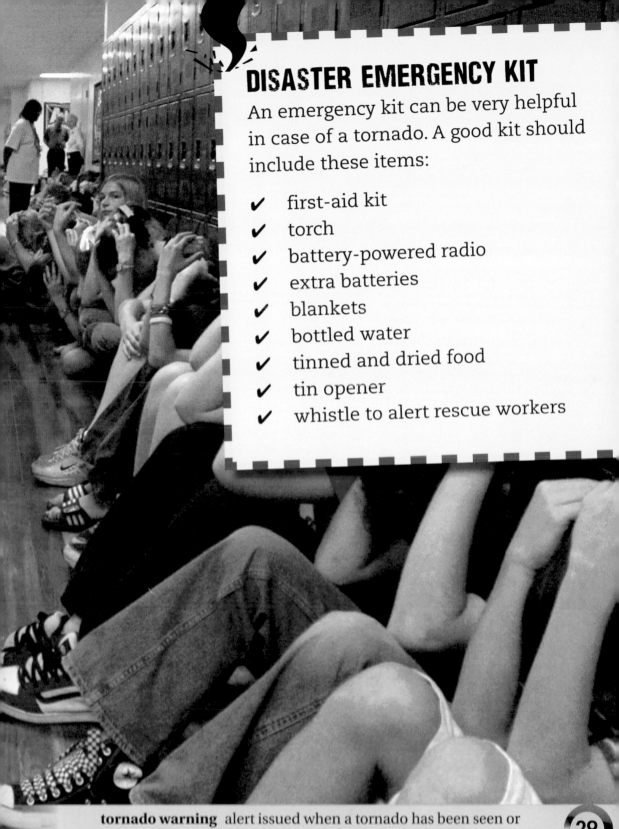

DISASTER EMERGENCY KIT

An emergency kit can be very helpful in case of a tornado. A good kit should include these items:

- ✔ first-aid kit
- ✔ torch
- ✔ battery-powered radio
- ✔ extra batteries
- ✔ blankets
- ✔ bottled water
- ✔ tinned and dried food
- ✔ tin opener
- ✔ whistle to alert rescue workers

tornado warning alert issued when a tornado has been seen or is expected soon

GLOSSARY

cyclone fast spinning column of air

debris scattered pieces of something that has been broken or destroyed

hail small pellets of ice that can fall during a thunderstorm

humid having a high level of water vapour in the air

hurricane very large storm with high winds and rain that forms over an ocean

outbreak large number of events that occur in a certain area

tornado warning alert issued when a tornado has been seen or is expected soon

READ MORE

Hurricane and Tornado (Eyewitness), Jack Challoner (DK Children, 2014)

Surviving Tornadoes (Children's True Stories: Natural Disasters), Elizabeth Raum (Raintree, 2012)

Tornadoes: Be Aware and Prepare (Weather Aware), Martha E. H. Rustad (Capstone Press, 2015)

WEBSITES

www.dkfindout.com/uk/earth/weather/effects-extreme-weather

Find out more about the extreme effects of weather.

www.ngkids.co.uk/science-and-nature/tornado-facts

Ten tornado facts to discover!

COMPREHENSION QUESTIONS

1. Tornadoes often kill people and cause huge amounts of damage. Which tornado was the deadliest in history? Which one was the costliest?

2. Explain what you would do if you heard a tornado warning.

3. Look at the chart on pages 4–5. What are the wind speeds for each category of tornado on the EF scale?

INDEX